The Journey

First published 2019

Copyright © H. Davies 2019

The right of H. Davies to be identified as the author of this work has been asserted in accordance with the Copyright, Designs & Patents Act 1988.

All rights reserved. No part of this book may be reproduced, stored in a retrieval system, or transmitted in any form or by any means, electronic, electrostatic, magnetic tape, mechanical, photocopying, recording or otherwise, without the written permission of the copyright holder.

Published under licence by Brown Dog Books and
The Self-Publishing Partnership, 7 Green Park Station, Bath BA1 1JB

www.selfpublishingpartnership.co.uk

ISBN printed book: 978-1-83952-074-7

Cover design by Kevin Rylands
Internal design by Andrew Easton

Printed and bound in the UK

This book is printed on FSC certified paper

The Journey

H. DAVIES

To the Woman
who is my mother in Truth

And in our pain
And confusion
We should know
That our darkness
Is only light
We cannot see
Which veils
Our understanding

CONTENTS

Page	
10	The Beginning
13	The Harmony of Life
14	The Wall
18	The Ghost of Fear
19	The Child
20	The Gift
21	The Legacy
22	The Question
23	The Clothes
24	The Fourth Decade
25	The Friend
26	The Chains
27	The Present
28	The Visit
29	The Emptiness
30	The Stranger
31	The Mute
32	The Masquerade
33	The Cleaving
34	The Frost
35	The Rest
36	The Girls

37 The Cry
38 The Letter
39 The Crime
40 The Yoke
41 The Battle
42 The Giant
43 The Funeral
44 The Jailer
45 The Sadness
46 The Fury
47 The Assertion
48 The Impotence
49 The Wait
50 The Truth Revealed
51 The Living Dead
52 Behold
53 The Cry
54 The Truth
55 The Messages
56 The Journey
58 The Holy Traveller

PROLOGUE

I was born in London during the war in 1942. My mother and father lived in Clapham near to the very busy Clapham railway junction which was a prime target for the German bombers.

My mother was a bag of nerves – understandably, as an invasion was on the cards. She was evacuated to Northampton where I was born.

When I was two I was put into a children's home whilst my brother John was born. I had only one visitor during my stay there.

I imagine that I was not impressed when I got home to find a baby boy! Moreover, it was a baby boy who took all my parents' time, as he cried incessantly. This was at a time when I desperately needed my mother – especially in view of my stay at the children's home which was traumatic. I have no memory of the children's home but the trauma was buried deep.

When I was about three I had to go into hospital to have a small operation. My mother sat on a chair opposite a nurse, talking, and it soon became apparent to me that I was there to stay. I ran away, hiding under the nurse's table, but was carried away, screaming. I can remember the big nurse who took off my clothes and put me in a bath. She was washing me and talking to me. My mother said she could hear me screaming all the way down the street!

Fast-forward to when I had my first child, and my 40-year struggle with depression for which various doctors prescribed various anti-depressants until I moved to my present house and met a GP who eventually suggested that I had psychotherapy…

....

I saw my psychotherapist once a week for four years from 1985. It was during this time that the poems in this book came to me in the way that dreams come to us from the unconscious. I was not aware of composing them – they emerged fully formed.

As the poems came to me, I would take them to therapy sessions where my therapist and I would explore them, and the meaning in them, together.

Through this process I was able to become aware of things from my past I had been unaware of until then.

As we know, the psyche cleverly protects us from trauma by burying memory and allowing us to disassociate from it until we are ready to bear it, which is what psychotherapy can help with.

The Beginning

'I wish this child had never been born'
The baby knew
But kept the pain inside.

'Nowhere for her to go – the war is on'
The child is taken from sleep
To a home.
Strangers – no father – no mother
No warning – no explanation – no hope.
Abandoned
And fearful
And silent.
The child knew
But kept the pain inside.

A baby brother – how did the child feel?
The war rages on – the baby cries and cries.
Mother and Father cope
Best they may.
And the child is forgotten.

Father's love for his small daughter
Threatens Mother.

No more love.
The child knows
But keeps the pain inside.

Childhood spent happily
Outside the house.
Inside all is torment.
Parents hate – silent atmospheres reign.
And the children suffer
Silently.

One brother loved by Mother
The other by Father.
Then there is the child from the home.
The mother is able to hide her jealous dislike
No longer.
'Who do you think will look at you?'
'You're useless – untidy – no good.'

The girl listens and knows
But keeps the pain inside

And all through my life
The pain stayed inside.
Until now.
Now I walk around full of tears.
So angry at times
I can taste it.
Unable to measure the pain.
So tired and frightened
And sad
But hoping one day to be free.

The Harmony of Life

I can only play with my left hand
The low notes
The sad notes.
My right hand doesn't play
The notes of joy
And happiness
To make a harmony.

For happiness spells
Danger
And joy makes me
Vulnerable.

I am always on my guard
Against any breach
In my defences.
I shore them up with
Criticism, disgust
And hostility.

So my right hand remains still,
Fearful of the high notes…
Denying harmony.

The Wall

A child sits on the floor
In the corner
Fists clenched
In pain and fear.

Around her is a wall
Which she had built
With two-year-old hands,
Made of glass blocks
Which looked like ice
Cemented with uncomprehending hurt.

The wall was mighty
And on it printed the words
'I do not need your love'
Which could be read
By those who came close enough.

The wall was a magical wall –
Nobody knew it was there
Nobody came close enough
To read the words.
Even the girl forgot
Though it kept her safe
And secure.
Behind the wall

In safety
The girl had a box
Into which she put
All the unlove,
The pain, the loneliness
The hurt and the loss.
And these too she forgot.

And so she grew up
Keeping the child safe.
Until one day she met
A man.
Love.
The child stepped through the wall
And blossomed.
Until…
Pregnant – vulnerable again.
Ill – homeless.
The man couldn't help her
But the wall could.

The box behind the wall
Was so full
The child was worried about it
And a woman came
Who knew about the box
And the wall.

She and the child
Looked and looked
Until they found the key
And they opened the box.
The woman sat
While the child slowly
Painfully
Started to empty the box.

The child never knew
A box
Could hold so much.
So many tears
So much pain
But as each thing was removed
The child and the woman
Looked at it together
Then threw it away
And the child felt
Much more comfortable
And had room to grow.

But the wall remains
Strong
Protective
And the child is not happy
Alone
Behind the wall.

With furious anger
She guards the wall.
The anger a mask
To hide the fear.

Without the wall
The girl will be naked
Vulnerable again.
She will have to reach out
To others
For her happiness.

Only she can take her wall down
The wall which now makes her unhappy
But which still keeps her safe.
She doesn't know how
Or if she can.

The Ghost of Fear

I am gripped by mortal fear –
Like a dying person
Frantically clinging
To life.

Unable to rest
Tense
Agitated
Angry and distressed
Inwardly screaming
I can't
I won't

Terrified
In the face of the
Inevitable.

Yet I know
I must pass through
From the life I know
To what I am told is
A better life…

Tomorrow

The Child

If we could see
The child behind the mask
We would wonder
At his frailty;
Our hearts would be touched
By his pain
And his doubts;
We would be moved
By his reasoning
And we would stand in awe
At the grandeur of his being.

If we could see
The child behind the mask
We would be kind.

The Gift

Bound by the past
I cannot move forwards
I cannot move backwards
Trapped
Soul weary
In my struggle for freedom
Which continues
Relentless.
My life seems over
I feel I am dying
Inside.

I look back
On my wasted life
Withered
Sterile
Devoid of all
Powerful emotions.
Tightly banded
By self-control.
God – the sadness
The regret.

I look at my children
Growing
Achieving independence.
I hope they will be free
To laugh
To cry
To be.

Treasure the love I have for you
My sons
It is gift
It is all.

The Legacy

The young man read
His mother's words
And the knowledge within
Was revealed.
His anger
His pain
His loneliness
Came forth –
Raw
Painful
Shocking him.

His mother watched
The pain in his eyes,
Helpless
Guilty
Her heart breaking.

Scenes of his young life
Haunting her
Condemning
Searing her soul.

If only…
If I could have another chance
If I knew then
What I know now.
But… too late
The legacy has been
Passed on.

But this will be the
Last generation.
We will conquer.
We will break the chain.

The Question

Who am I?
Did I just forget
Or have I never known?

Did I get lost
Under the needs of others
Living for them –
Now living through them.

Are the invisible cords
That bind me to my husband
To my sons
Of my own making
Of my own choosing?
Am I frightened that
Without them
There will be no reason
For my existence?

I must be a person…
Everybody else is.

The Clothes

The girl was growing
And her clothes were becoming
Uncomfortable
Restricting.

And she thought she saw
Some new clothes nearby –
Yellow and green
As the fields in spring;
Blue as the wide, open sky;
Dappled as sunlight
Dancing on the leaves.

And the girl knew
That if she wore these
New clothes
She would feel
Freer
Happier… but

She tightly clasped
Her rags around her.
'If I wore these new clothes'
She pondered
Fearful
'Perhaps I would no longer belong
With those I have loved.
Perhaps I shall have to
Go away.'

Or maybe
Her freedom would grow
Within her.

The Fourth Decade

A child
Unloved
Overcome by pain
Gives up.
Light slowly dims
And is gone.

A child
Unloved
Overcome by pain
Lives –
Her need
Encapsulated
In ice.

Now in her
Fourth decade
She understands;
The ice must melt –
The need must
Painfully emerge,
And what she has
So vehemently denied
Must be embraced.

The Friend

I saw pain approaching from afar,
And trembled;
I filled every silence to keep her away,
But she would not be denied.

Her touch was hard to bear;
Her presence –
Loneliness,
Her words –
Despair.

She embraced me –
I could not sleep
For pain;
My bones ached
My heart was pierced.
Her cruelty seemed endless.

And still she keeps me company,
Her power
Undiminished.
No longer a foe
To be feared,
But a dear friend
To be trusted.
For I turned to look
And saw her face
And beheld that she was
Me.

The Chains

The girl wanted to fly
To soar into
Her own being;
To the joy of oneness
With herself.
But her feet were chained
Held fast
To the ground.
Each link of the chain
Forged from ancient hurts
And present fears.

Now flapping her wings
Desperate to be free,
Now drooping in despair
At her futile struggle.
She cannot find a way to break free.

The Present

The lonely girl
Was given a present.
It was a golden ball.
Light as thistledown
It glowed and shone;
Beautiful.
It filled her soul with joy.

She carried it
Wherever she went,
Afraid to put it down
To admire it
In case she lost it.

Gradually it became
Awkward to carry –
It hampered her movements
And stopped her doing
What she wanted to do.
But she didn't complain
For fear of offending
He who gave her
The present.

As time went by
The ball lost its glow
And became dull,
Boring.
It grew heavier and heavier
Until she resented its presence.
She began to hate it
And wanted to put it down.

Having put it down,
Would she again be left
With nothing?

The Visit

The Lady Julian
Bade me welcome –
We sat awhile.
Her blackbird sang
Unseen.
In the garden
At peace
I held my being
In gentle solitude.

The Emptiness

Where is the unshadowed star
That should be mine,
To comfort
And illume
In dark
And troubled times?

At what altar
Do I kindle
The flame of self-worth
To warm
The emptiness?

The Stranger

Anger
Is a stranger
In my mansion;
She dwells
In distant chambers
Unwanted
Disregarded.

She haunts my ways;
If she appears,
Eyes full of words
Lips contorted,
I slam my door
And flee headlong.

Undaunted
She wafts
Into my rooms
Unbidden,
Unseen,
Permeating
Oppressing
Clouding my vision
Stultifying my senses.

Poor, mute Anger –
If only she could speak
She would be free
To leave.

The Mute

The girl had learned
Her lesson
Well.
'We do not want
To hear your voice' –
So she trained herself
Not to speak.

In obedient silence
She lived her life,
Certain that her voice
Was dangerous;
Fearful
That those who heard it,
Being so hurt,
Would want to
Die.

And now her feelings
Need to speak…
But she has forgotten
The words.

The Masquerade

I should like to
Remove my mask.
I am weary
Of holding it
In place.

But the masked revellers,
Waltzing serenely,
Whirling gaily,
Would recoil;
My unmasked features
A discomforting
Disrupting
Reminder.
For dancers
Do not welcome
Naked faces.

So I must remain
Hidden;
Mask adjusted
Anguish concealed –
My fight for life
Within.

The Cleaving

I fought for the girl;
I picked up the tiny form.
I held her tight
I smashed the glass
I SCREAMED.

Gradually,
As we clung
One to another,
Her memories became
Mine,
The fear and horror
Ours.

The Frost

The springtime in my heart
My tide of joy
Are stayed –
Suspended in
Silent deference
To a frosty covering
Of fear.

Should springtime's balmy air
Be allowed,
My many layers,
Worn to protect
Against winter's chill,
Must needs be
Discarded.
My naked form
Would be enveloped
In the warmth of the sun,
And the ice in my veins
Would melt.
Without the burden
Of ungainly clothes
I would dance and twirl –
My heart would sing.

BUT
'Remember'
Says the snake
'once before
Long ago
You were happy
In the sun;
You danced
In its warmth,
And in the midst
Of your
Unsuspecting happiness
I killed you.'

The Rest

Here on this hillside,
In the shadow
Of an ancient church
Which stands,
Thatched and still,
Keeping prayerful watch
Over field and hedge,
I hope one day
To rest.

Freed at last
From the need to belong,
My spirit shall soar
On the wing of the lark;
Hand in hand with the wind
I shall sweep the fields –
Poppies and corn
Will dip their heads before us;
I shall melt into
The dappled coolness
Of the greenwood,
And I shall fill the sky
With my song of joy –
My song of me.

The Girls

In my dreams
Through the mists of time
Came three small girls.

The first
Black and merry –
So pleased to see me.
Happily we laughed together.

The second
An urchin,
Small and tousled.
She clung fast to me
Declaring
'I'm tough, I am.'
My hot tears
Washed our faces –
For I knew her hurt
And anger.

The third
Timid and trembling,
So full of fear.
Forbidden to speak
By the man;
Hemmed in by his
Angry presence…
How I mourn for this child,
Saddened by her distress.
I wanted to take her in my arms,
Enfold her misery
In my love.
But she is gone
Leaving me with such a
Heavy heart.

The Cry

I look at myself – I see
An essence
Without form;
A being
Without purpose.
An aching heart
A faceless soul.
Oh God
Where do I find
My identity.

The Letter

My dear, dear son –
How your suffering
Cuts me.
If I could take your pain
I would.
How can I help you?
I can only hold you,
Be with you
Whilst childhood's
Sad and bitter memories
Wrack your being.

Let flow your tears of anger,
Allow the tears of your heart –
Their salty balm will heal.
Do not be afraid
For they will not
Quench my love for you.

Take in your arms
The small, unhappy boy
Who walks
In your shadow,
And hold him close.
Kiss him,
Reassure him,
Give him all the love
His tormented mother
Could not give.

The Crime

You stand accused
Of murder.
You killed me.
At one blow
You destroyed my trust.
You strangled the tender shoots
Of my identity,
Robbed me of love
And left me bleeding.

Your partner,
Your accomplice,
Who had no mouth
Or eyes
Was cold –
No succour there!
No mother's kisses
Or protecting arms,
Just thinly veiled dislike
And acid tongue
Which burned
Emerging life.

Both found guilty
Of killing your child,
But no sentence can be passed
No punishment given –
For a life sentence
Has already been served.

The Yoke

The yoke around my shoulders
The childhood burden
Of pleasing
Has bent my back.
In my quest
Never to annoy
Or oppose
I stooped
And saw only the ground.

Now I must straighten
My stiffened spine
And look at the world,
And the world
Will look at me.

The Battle

Frustrated
Angry
I want to scream
I want to cry –
But what's the point?

I cannot reach
The hidden torment
Guarded well by some
Subconscious sentinel.

I battle and strive
To know,
But the blank wall
Of protective fear
Defies me.

I endeavour therefore
To enjoy my days;
To ignore the whirling thoughts.
I deserve happiness.
I have the right
To relax in the sun,
To enjoy the peace
Which must come
When mind and body
Are at rest.

But happiness cannot be willed
Nor peace demanded.
I must continue to journey
Through the depths of my being.
I must walk the dark ways –
Open long-rusted locks
And confront
The past events
Which are killing
My today.

The Giant

Beneath deep dungeons
Lies a subterranean pit –
A seething mass of fury,
Spitting red-hot anger
High into the air,
Spewing destructive wrath.

The sleeping giant
Who dwells therein
Begins to stir.
Steel-hard eyes
Filled with loathing,
Lips curled with malice,
He shouts.
His roars fill the sky –
'I despise your weakness.
I like to watch you suffer;
You shall wither before my gaze
And my scorn will char your bones.'

The world was shaken
And all song was silenced.

The Funeral

I sit in the garden
By the pond
In the rain
Sobbing my grief
To the darkness

Today I stood
At the graveside,
My shoulder wet
With mother's tears.

I have met all needs,
Dry-eyed I have supported;
Unflagging I coped.
No one saw my hurts
And needs –
Nor will they.

I will not allow them
To see me
Naked
In my vulnerability.
So I sit alone
In the dark.

The Jailer

'They will not make me cry'
My childhood vow declared,
And my infant mind
Quietly
Purposefully
Raised a barrier.
They could not make me
Feel the pain!

Now I want to feel my feelings;
To meet with sorrow and with joy.
To rediscover deep felt needs,
Tenderness and trust.
But my mind,
My long-time protector
So strong and sure,
Is now my jailer –
Keeping me,
Puzzled and frustrated,
From the fullness and freedom
Of my own being.

The Sadness

The air is still
Time holds its breath.
In the autumn of the year
In the autumn of my life
I begin to emerge;
I catch a glimpse
Of who I am
And am filled with sadness
For all the sadness.

The Fury

My tortured muscles
Bear witness to the strength
Of my fury.

My selfhood has been ignored
And my soul is outraged.

You have not acknowledged
My separate existence,
My unique personality.
You have not looked at me.

Do not deny
Nor expect me to consider
Sensibly
All the reasons why.
For now, just stand
In the light of the truth,
And allow me the dignity
Of my anger.

The Assertion

No, it isn't alright;
How could you have violated
My infant self,
My trusting love.

No, it isn't alright;
You crippled
My inner freedom,
Paralysing my being
And freezing my capacity
To enjoy and be happy.
You filled me with blackness
And despair.
No, damn you
It isn't alright.

The Impotence

'I don't care what you think
Or how you feel about it –
This is how it's going to be.
I will do just as I please
Whether you like it or not.
I dismiss with contempt
Your protestations
And laugh at your complaints.'

No one listens to me.
With tears of helpless anger
I rage
And beat the walls
With fists of impotence.

I hate men
They impose their will
Uncaring
Hard
Expecting no resentment
Brooking no defiance.

And if I dare
To voice my grievance
One look
Evaporates my words –
My reasoning is scattered
All logic is gone.

I am not mad!
I am demented
In my fury
But I am not mad!

The Wait

Quietly the woman sits
And waits for me to break.

When failed by those
Who should have loved,
And left unprotected
When in need;
When my trusting love
Was trampled underfoot,
I did not break!

When paralysed with fear
In strange surroundings;
When nowhere was safe,
No person to be trusted;
When affection was dangerous
And loneliness a way of life,
I did not break.

Oh yes, I see
I understand.
I know the tears would free me
And the pain release;
Clearly I see the division within
But angrily I say
They will not break me.

The Truth Revealed

The girl's clothes
Had worn out,
But she covered herself
With a blanket of confidence
And the cloak of ambition.

The winds of circumstance had tugged
And dragged at her covers,
But the girl hugged them to her.
The winds increased –
Tearing at her cloak
Whipping the blanket to shreds.
The girl's body ached
As she clung vainly
To her protection.

What a poor thing was revealed
When the last threads
Were blown away.
The girl shivered in her nakedness,

And cried with shame
As the world beheld
The pain of her hurt,
Saw the reality of her fear,
Her weakness
And her very littleness.

The Living Dead

'You have so much to offer –
You have ability
Intelligence
Understanding
You can succeed.'

Thank you.
I know you mean well,
And I have tried;
But something inside
Undermines –
Will not allow.

What you didn't see
And I but vaguely comprehend
Is the black child.
She is the one
People didn't want to know.
Ridiculed
Ignored
Best forgotten!

The child so black with anger
Rage
And seething indignation
Buried herself
And lay quiet.
Thinking she had no right
To exist.

But she will be ignored no longer
And will stop all movement –
All progress;
Will allow no achievement
Until she is seen and accepted,
Listened to with respect
And loved.

Behold

Behold the child.
Blind and deaf
Undeveloped
Handicapped
Isolated
Unreachable.

Only touch her
Love her
Reach her
And she will amaze
As, all untutored
She plays Brahms.

The Cry

In the depth of your need
You walked through the night
To my door.
Silently screaming, 'Wake up!'
You rang the bell.
I did not hear!

In your darkest hour
You were knocking
And I heard nothing!

You came to me – hurting
Needing the comfort
Of one who understood,
But I did not wake.
I did not hear you
I did not hear me.

NB a young friend of my son, whose mother had recently died, was knocking on the door one night in great distress. No one heard her!

The Truth

At last – the hidden conviction
That by which I lived
Imprisoned –
Is revealed.
'You are not good enough.'

My inner battle
Which quietly raged
Using so much energy
Causing so much tension
So many sleepless nights.
Was the fight against
'You are not good enough.'

Doubting my abilities
Working and struggling
I did it all
In my head –
Not trusting myself to be
In case I heard
'You are not good enough.'

Now I am free
To value myself,
To see myself as alright –
No better or worse than others –
But good enough.

The Messages

'Don't make that noise –
You'll disturb other children.'
'Big girls don't cry.
That's enough of that noise.'
When will be the right time
When acceptable
To feel my deepest feelings?

'Nobody wants your temper –
It will get you into trouble one day.'
'Don't get out of your pram.'
They laughed and jeered at my rage.
When will be the right time
When acceptable
To feel my deepest feelings?

'Don't be so silly.'
'Keep your voice down.'
'Cheer up, misery.'
'Put a smile on your face.'
When will be the right time
When acceptable
To feel my deepest feelings?

Denied pain cutting me in half
Uncontrollable shaking and tears;
Friends would say
'Are you often like this?'
When will be the right time
When acceptable
To feel my deepest feelings?

Therapy – reaching the pain
Dam ready to burst –
'Time to stop' –
'It's ten to five.'
When will be the right time
When acceptable
To feel my deepest feelings?

The Journey

The girl had travelled far,
Was almost naked
And so, so weary.

She sat on a rock
And pondered her journey.
She had seen some terrible things
And felt fear and despair
Such as could not be described.

When she had first set out
Across the lonely wastes
Of unforgiving desert
With no drop of water
To refresh,
She had not guessed
What mountains of adversity,
What ravines of pain
Lay in the darkness ahead,

She had not known
Of the plateaux of nothingness
Which spanned the weeks;
Of the pass between high rocks
Which she, with rising hopes,
Had trod –
Only to find a wall so vast
That it blotted out the sky.
She had beat her fists on the rock
Her screams echoing from granite face
To granite face.

But she had persevered,
Had found new paths
Through the inhospitable mountains
Which she had patiently climbed –
Hoping each mountain
Would be the last,
Only to see another peak
Shrouded in brooding mists.

There had been times
When all hopes seemed to have
fled –
Her strength gone,
And she had wanted to die.

Now at last her exile had ended.
She had reached a place
Where people lived.
Walking through the cold streets
She had been drawn
Like a moth
To the lighted windows
Through which she gazed with
longing,
Hoping to find her home;
The place where she belonged.

Her eyes had searched the faces
Of those who had passed by –
Where was her mother?
Now surely she would find
The one who would love and
cherish,
Comfort and restore her wounded
soul.
She, whose mother-love and
acceptance
Would be a home within a home.

Tears slowly fell
From the eyes
Of the girl on the rock.

The wind grew colder
And its chill caught her heart.
She shuddered.
The thought slowly came –
Perhaps she would never
Find her home.

The Holy Traveller

The holy man
And the traveller
Met
And tarried awhile.

'Have you found God
In all your wanderings?'
The holy man asked,
His wise eyes
Gazing peacefully
At the traveller.

'I have searched,'
Cried the traveller.
'All my life I have prayed
That I might find God –
But to no avail.
Now I rely only
On myself.'

The holy man spoke again.
'God is always with me;
He guides my ways.
If I listen to Him
In prayer.'

The traveller thought long
And replied
'In the solitude
Of my journeyings
I have learned to listen
To myself
And have learned much.'

Together they watched
As the day dimmed;
In silence
The night's darkness
Enfolded them.

'When I am weak
I ask God for strength'
The holy man continued
'He never fails me.'

'When I meet trouble
I somehow find strength
From deep within,'
Pondered the traveller.

The holy man smiled
'I know that God loves me
And I am filled with His peace.
Would that I could share
That joy with you.'

'Ah,' laughed the traveller
'Being at peace with myself
Is the greatest joy I know.'

That night
In his dreams
The traveller beheld
A great tree
Laden with fruit –
The tree spoke to him
Saying
'Son of man,
Whence think you
Comes my fruit –
From me
Or from the earth
Which encloses my roots?'

In the morning
The holy traveller,
Having understood,
Went on his way
Rejoicing.